Prompt Me More
Creative Writing Journal & Workbook

Prompt Me Series #2

By
Robin Woods

Epic Books Publishing

A boutique publishing company
Visit us at: www.epicbookspublishing.com

Editor: Beth Braithwaite

Copyright © 2017 Robin Woods
First Edition

Cover Design created on Canva by Robin Woods

All Photos taken by Robin Woods

Fonts: Century, Gothic Ultra

Summary: A wide variety of writing prompts for maximum inspiration.

[Creative Writing, Diary, Non-Fiction, Reference, Writing Workbook, Fiction Writing, Writing Journal]

ISBN-10: 1-941077-11-0
ISBN-13: 978-1-941077-11-5

Table of Contents

Introduction

When taking pictures for this workbook, I came across this stacked wood in a wild array of colors. Part of it reminded me of a pile of books and the other part of an artist's palette—wild hues in haphazard designs that were used to create something else very beautiful. That is much like writing.

Writing is sometimes messy, and sometimes we need a little help even getting to the mess. When you begin to form your ideas, don't worry about grammar and punctuation. Simply getting the words down and experimenting is the most important part in the beginning. In order to become a better writer, you need to do three things:

1. Write often.

2. Read often.

3. Don't be afraid to make mistakes.

Embrace the mess, find your voice, and don't get discouraged. As Earnest Hemingway once said:

"There is nothing to writing. All you do is sit down at a typewriter and bleed."

Think of these pages as your artist's studio. Experiment with color and style. You never know; you may start something that grows into a masterpiece.

How to Use This Book

There are a variety of different styles of prompts in this workbook to help you decide what works best for you. If one style or prompt doesn't work, move on. If it doesn't work for you today, it might tomorrow.

If the pronouns don't work for you, change the she to a he, or vice versa. Prompts are meant to be inspiration, not shackles.

Carry it around with you. Mess it up. Use different kinds of ink. Stick Post-Its all over it.

Now, go forth and write!

Picture Prompts

It has often been said that a picture is worth a thousand words—but that doesn't really help writers. However, a picture can inspire thousands of words.

Use the following photos to create a unique story.

1. Title: _____

2. Title: _____

4. Title: _____

5. Title: _____

6. Title: _____

7. Title: _____

8. Title: _____

9. Title: _____

10. Title: _____

11. Title: _____

12. Title: _____

13. Title: _____

14. Title: _____

15. Title: _____

Story Starters:
First Person

Emotional Standpoint: Subjective
View: Limited
Pronoun Usage: I/we/us/me/my/mine/our/ours

Writing Challenge:

Limit the amount of times your character "felt" or "feels" something. Use active voice to help keep the reader in the experience.

First Person

16. Pushing the small vial towards me, he said, "Drink this. I need to know the truth."

17. As I stared at the last of the embers flitting in the wind like crazed fireflies, I shrugged with the epiphany: I was the villain in this story.

18. There was no way. Me, the President? Ha.

19. The creak of the floorboard in front of my room had my heart in a sprint. Carefully, I slid the sheets to the side...

20. But they had promised! I glowered down at the empty envelope, hands shaking. Only one path was open to me now...

21. My image, I realized, was totally romanticized; pirates smelled atrocious in person—and they definitely needed a better dental plan.

22. Were there any honest people left in the world? Then, I remembered...

23. The horizon itself began to bow and twist, then I noticed...

24. A fresh coat of snow crunched under my heavy boots. I heaved a breath as I surveyed...

25. My back creaked and groaned after sleeping behind the dumpster...

26. The last time I saw my father, the wind was so loud that I thought Zeus himself had...

27. The door burst open, sending my papers into a flurry onto the floor. This was the last time...

28. He was a good liar, I almost believed him...for about three seconds.

29. *He was my king*. I pushed away the thought nagging in the back of my brain...

30. "It may sound cliché, but I haven't told anyone this before," I said as I tried to swallow past the lump in my throat...

31. When the egg hatched, saying it wasn't what I'd expected couldn't begin to explain...

32. I sprinted from gravestone to gravestone, my terror raking icy fingers down my spine.

33. Running my hand down the fireproof panel, I hoped it was as flame resistant as the salesperson assured.

34. Everyone was gone. The only option I had was to start walking...

35. The crack-clack-clack started to get to me. How many more hours would...

36. My coworker observed me sitting alone at the table, but chose to snub me and sit at another table—alone.

37. Though I recognized her, the thing smiling from behind her eyes was...

38. When I opened the napkin the waitress had dropped off, there was a note that said, "Slowly exit the back door now. It's your only hope."

39. I caught them staring again, but this time, I held my ground and stared back.

40. As we gazed at the night sky, the stars seemed to be growing closer.

41. The air was too thick. Panting, I waved at the medic—stars flashed and my vision started to narrow as...

42. No matter what I tried, the glitter wouldn't come off, and I only had minutes before...

43. I kept repeating the only Morse code I knew. S...O...S...

44. The stupid garden gnome was on my porch again.

45. Happiness swelled inside me and went supernova within seconds. This was...

46. My grandfather told me that books are as important as weapons. Clearly, this was...

47. Giggles kept bubbling out of us like a stupid babbling brook. We covered our mouths to try to stifle them.

48. There was a reason that the number thirteen was my favorite. A secret smile curled the edge of my mouth.

49. The hot cheese stuck to the roof of my mouth when...

50. This was not how I'd pictured my wedding day. I glanced surreptitiously at the armed men at every exit before...

51. Lights were draped around the room like a thousand tiny stars that seemed to be calling to me. Surely my destiny was about to be revealed...

52. The guy at the auto parts store gawked at me like I was wearing a straightjacket and spouting conspiracy theories.

53. My eyes bulged. "Don't you recognize an empty noble gesture when you hear it?"

54. He was dead—not sick as I'd been told. Dark emotion rattled around inside my ribcage before the first...

55. His kindness humbled me. How had I been so arrogant...and entitled? I grabbed paper and started to scrawl...

56. At first, the air appeared to shimmer. Then I realized it was millions of tiny, green insects swarming...

57. It had to be a cat—I think. I followed the sound, each step quiet as to not eclipse...

58. I tore at the paper and managed to papercut my palm. Fantastic—yet another crowning achievement for today.

59. "Make something amazing," she'd told me. I stuck my tongue out at her retreating figure, and then glared back at the ingredients.

60. "I'm a rat," I finally admitted. "Before you say anything, know it's true."

61. He shoved the ring roughly onto my finger, but I suppressed the yelp. Then he said, "Keep this on; it will protect you."

62. They thought I would fear the dark. My grin spread wide—this is what I had been waiting for.

63. My lungs clattered with each cough, making me feel like a dented cow bell.

64. His stare made me feel guilty even though I hadn't done anything wrong. I could win an award for the world's most boring person. Well, until last night that is.

65. "So, this is like a transporter from *Star Trek* or something?" I asked.

66. Somebody was lying, that much was obvious. I sucked on a tooth while deliberating. One of my frenemies was about to become...

67. My toes curled in the too-small shoes, making it difficult to traverse the...

68. Lightning splintered the tree to my left as I foundered in the mud. I willed my legs to move faster, but...

69. Easing the drawer out, I found it was full of doll parts—the creepy variety.

70. I'd been anticipating this kiss for months, but his lips were too firm and he had too much saliva in his mouth. *Eww. Was it possible to be this bad of a kisser?*

71. The moment I was sworn in, I was shuffled into a room teaming with...

72. Fish were bobbing on the surface of the pool looking semi-translucent and rubbery. I fought with the urge to dry heave from the stench, but then I might lose my footing...

73. Best. Day. Ever. The pep in my step bordered on skipping as...

74. Dragging a dead body behind me was way harder in real life. Maybe I should've stretched first, or at least worn...

75. This is where you were murdered.

Prompt # _____ Your Title: _____

Prompt # _____ Your Title: _____

_____

_____

_____

_____

_____

_____

_____

_____

_____

_____

_____

_____

_____

_____

_____

_____

_____

_____

_____

_____

_____

_____

_____

_____

_____

_____

_____

Prompt # _____ Your Title: _____

Prompt # _____ Your Title: _____

_____

_____

_____

_____

_____

_____

_____

_____

_____

_____

_____

_____

_____

_____

_____

_____

_____

_____

_____

_____

_____

_____

_____

Prompt # _____ Your Title: _____

Prompt # _____ Your Title: _____

Prompt # _____ Your Title: _____

Prompt # _____ Your Title: _____

Prompt # _____ Your Title: _____

Prompt # _____ Your Title: _____

Prompt # _____ Your Title: _____

Story Starters: Third Person

Third Person Limited
Emotional Standpoint: Objective
View: Limited
Pronoun Usage: he/she/it/him/his/her/they/their

Third Person Omniscient
Emotional Standpoint: Objective
View: Unlimited
Pronoun Usage: he/she/it/him/his/her/they/their

Deep Third Person
Emotional Standpoint: Subjective
View: Limited
Pronoun Usage: he/she/it/him/his/her/they/their

Writing Challenge:

Vary your language, especially your sentence openings. I.e. Not every sentence should begin with "The" or "Then."

Third Person

76. The honed steel went singing through the air, finding its mark. The invaders dove...

77. She grabbed the ringing phone, cringing at the number.

    A deep voice on the other end said, "Moriarty's Pizza. Your order is ready."

78. A concussive gong had him covering his ears, running...

79. She narrowed her eyes at him. "You see my coffee cup? I cannot guarantee your safety if you speak to me before it's empty."

80. The weight in the hold made the whole ship groan. He wiped sweat from his brow as he...

81. When she examined the postmark, she immediately pulled out gloves and a mask before handling the envelope further.

82. *The sand was everywhere*, he thought while sifting...

83. She could smell the flowers before she opened the door. Her worst nightmare was in the next room. The second she turned the knob...

84. Aunt Agatha was the town oracle—he prayed she was wrong.

85. When his code name flashed on the screen in front of him, his bowels went watery. They knew.

86. White fluttered to the ground all around them. At first, they believed it to be snow, but...

87. She woke when the steady hum of the night creatures came to an abrupt stop and was replaced by eerie silence.

88. The inky black spread as if some terrible monster was creating it, but...

89. Serial killers often keep tokens from their victims—she bought a charm for each life she saved.

90. He plugged the earbuds into his ears and cranked the volume to block the flood of...

91. Reading the survival guide books he'd purchased over the years would have been a good idea. He ferreted out one of the few herbs he'd remembered before...

92. "*Officially* apologize?" They would be lucky if she didn't file "official" charges.

93. They scoffed at the protestors scurrying around on the street below. If they only knew what they had truly triggered.

94. The words teetered on the tip of her tongue for longer than they should have, but then...

95. When their eyes met, the world seemed to fall away—or maybe it had.

96. He clutched his heart, the pain shooting down his left arm—they'd done it.

97. "Easy for you," he accused. "All you have to do is sit there and look scary. They expect me to be the brains of this...whatever you want to call it." With his jaw clenched, he started cramming items into his pack...

98. Cackling came from the darkness. "You have inherited his debt."

99. She was born a princess, but now she was a general, and no one was going to take this command from her. Strapping the armor...

100. The veil between worlds was thin this time of year. He gazed at the red moon...

101. He tucked the loose strands of hair behind her ear one last time. "I won't remember you tomorrow. Don't take it personally." The sensation always started at his brain stem, and then slithered along his nerves. It was starting early this time...

102. The text message read: "They aren't following you, they're following me."

103. She rolled her eyes and tried to keep her voice steady. "Who gets attacked by a raccoon on a boat? For reals, who does?"

104. She found out the hard way—assassins can't be trusted, even if they are your brother.

105. From below, the flutter of motion on top of the building appeared to be unsettled birds. But it wasn't...

106. He had seen her a thousand times in her dreams, he now regretted invading them.

107. Words swirled in his head. With the end of the world immanent, he had to tell her the truth.

108. They exchanged a look; the volcano was going to erupt, and they didn't have much time.

109. She spun in a circle while waving her hands in front of her, despite knowing that she looked silly.

110. Lights flashed passed the windows, fear trickled through his veins, and pricked at...

111. He tried to channel his inner Indiana Jones, but he felt more like the French guy who ate the fly and melted.

112. With a sharp yank, she tested the rope before repelling into the darkness...

113. His fingers grazed the handle of the gun shoved into his belt. Metal, warmed by his skin urged him to...

114. *It clearly didn't belong in a cage*, he thought, his fingers itching to grab the latch.

115. The muddy footprint on the windowsill was the only evidence.

116. Dust coated her tongue when she cried out, making the scorpion skitter to the side.

117. His lungs burned at the same time his vision narrowed into a blotchy tunnel. *Someone needs to stop me*, he thought.

118. Techno beats thrummed in the bodies of the writhing crowd, and lights flashed...

119. But the monster under her bed was her friend. For ages she'd reached down and stoked its scales as a form of self-soothing to drift off to sleep. But this sound was different...

120. Flowers unfurled as she walked past—even they were romanced by her presence.

121. Roadkill, recently scraped from the highway, was bubbling in the pot over the open flame, emitting gasps and gurgles...

122. The androids were stirring again.

123. Hungry blades of grass gobbled up the field. And when there was no more, they looked to the homes.

124. It wasn't a Girl Scout at the door selling cookies. She held her breath and froze.

125. As his grandma had told him, luck only lasted so long. This would have to be pure skill—no shock or surprise. They knew he was coming...

126. The world held its breath. The moment it blazed across the muddy sky leaving a trail...

127. Great yawning trees sighed to the side amongst those who were daring to take the pass. Amber light played in the trees, shifting with each clippity-clop of the horses.

128. *Piano music?* The airy tune streamed through the air vents, a whisper of beauty...

129. "It seems you have a hard time controlling your urges," the guard taunted. He wanted nothing more than a chance to test his skill against Prisoner 327.

130. The bracelets felt like shackles the moment she slipped into the grand ballroom.

131. "More terrifying than clowns?" he asked. "No, don't answer that. More terrifying than clowns holding dolls while covered in spiders?" Then he smirked.

132. Salt stung their eyes in great bursts of pain, blinding them to the approaching...

133. They all lived in a fishbowl, but it was time she used it to her advantage. She placed the note; it was hidden, but not too hidden...

134. The weight of his ancestors fell heavy on him. If he did this, there was no return...

135. It was her tenth birthday, and as with tradition, she would face the trials. She kept her pack light, only a few necessities, and one personal item...

Prompt # _____ Your Title: _____

Prompt # _____ Your Title: _____

Prompt # _____ Your Title: _____

Prompt # _____ Your Title: _____

_____
_____
_____
_____
_____
_____
_____
_____
_____
_____
_____
_____
_____
_____
_____
_____
_____
_____
_____
_____
_____
_____
_____
_____
_____
_____
_____
_____

Prompt # _____ Your Title: _____

Use These Phrases

Writing Challenge:

Writers often forget to incorporate the sense of smell into their writings. Try to use this sense in an offbeat way. There is a chart in the back to help with inspiration.

136. Choose and use at least six of these ten phrases:

held by rough hands	twisted lengths of rope
growing tension	bathed in amber light
exceptionally nervy	fog slithered
an unlikely savior	melted into the hug
sting of the cold	smoothed over her hips

137. Choose and use at least seven of these ten phrases:

a throb of light	rattle of machinery
with perfect contempt	scuffing of shoes
absence of sound	groan of metal
bone-deep chill	blistering commentary
smile outshined the heavens	empty inside

138. Choose and use at least eight of these ten phrases:

only described as portly	staunch the flow
a talisman of sorts	multitudinous wrongs
hide my elation	terror drained away
generosity of strangers	coiled like a snake
engulfed in flame	strangled sob

139. Choose and use at least nine of these ten phrases:

robust amount of confidence	delightful giggle
in close proximity	with a regal flourish
charming vulnerability	slashed in front of him
a grotesque array	harder than necessary
a complete invasion	searing honesty

140. Choose and use at least nine of these ten phrases:

triumphant moment	a plague plummeted
a meager portion	felt depraved
somehow seemed luxurious	the thirsty landscape
teetering on the edge	uncensored raw emotion
blossoming hope	a wry grin

Choose a Path

Writing Challenge:

Use at least three of the five senses in each of your stories.

☐ Sight ☐ Sound ☐ Hearing ☐ Taste ☐ Touch

If your story has fantasy elements, you can always add a sixth sense.

141. When the elevator opened,...

- ☐ it was nothing but an empty shaft.
- ☐ a SWAT team swarmed off, nearly trampling those waiting.
- ☐ rats scurried into the office, inciting a cacophony of screams.
- ☐ the tower of boxes the delivery person had, toppled to the floor.
- ☐ bloody handprints painted the back wall.

142. Slicing through the waves, the oncoming ship was filled with...

- ☐ refugees in need of help.
- ☐ party goers singing bad 80s music.
- ☐ fully armed coast guard members.
- ☐ a salvage crew in search of Atlantis.
- ☐ ghosts of the past.

_____

_____

_____

_____

_____

_____

_____

_____

_____

_____

_____

_____

_____

_____

_____

_____

_____

143. Smells wafted down the busy street,...

- ☐   mingling with car exhaust and despair.
- ☐   alerting unseen predators to fresh prey.
- ☐   the spices enticing the commuters.
- ☐   drawing members of the cockroach community.
- ☐   but no one noticed the bite of drugs over the odor of garbage.

144. The metal men...

- ☐ loomed above us as part of the giant sculpture.
- ☐ and women hosted a tea party.
- ☐ were bent on destruction.
- ☐ marched onto the cobblestone streets with torches.
- ☐ were part of a larger machine, spewing smoke as it moved away.

_____

_____

_____

_____

_____

_____

_____

_____

_____

_____

_____

_____

_____

_____

_____

_____

_____

145. Shadows danced...

- ☐ in the corners of the room, but didn't venture towards him.
- ☐ on the trees around the crackling bonfire.
- ☐ on the water like liquid serpents.
- ☐ as the children made shadow puppets in front of the lamp.
- ☐ on the tent during the savage storm.

146. Anxiety bloomed as assignments were...

□   passed back by the teacher.

□   given for the next group to be sent to the front lines.

□   hollered over the static on the comm.

□   divulged to the spy ring.

□   divided up amongst the marketing branch.

Dialogue Prompts

A few tips before we start:

- ☐ Avoid using the characters' names too much in dialogue.
- ☐ Make sure not all of your characters sound the same.
- ☐ Try not to have characters parrot or repeat the previous sentence.

Writing Challenge:

Use as few adverbs as possible.

☐ Generally, people don't speak in complete sentences. Use some fragments.
☐ Play with dialect and the way your characters use contractions.
☐ Restarts, stumbles, and stutters can improve emotional scenes.

147. "Explosives are my specialty," she grinned, tearing the tape off with her teeth.

"I prefer to be far, far away from objects that explode, smell bad, or spew anything. Unless it is spewing chocolate."

"Well, then. You are really going to hate this."

148. "Like…in space?"

"What else did you think I meant?" he shrugged.

She gasped, "ANYTHING, but that. Are you insane?""

_____

_____

_____

_____

_____

_____

_____

_____

_____

_____

_____

_____

_____

_____

_____

_____

_____

_____

_____

149. "Since you no longer respect or value human life, you are condemned to—"

"Hold up. You send me out to do the impossible. I do it. And now I'm in trouble?"

"In which level of hell would you like your reservation?"

She arched a manicured brow. "I plan on inheriting the whole thing.

150. "Is that my diary?"

"It sure isn't mine," he replied, with a slap-worthy smirk.

_____
_____
_____
_____
_____
_____
_____
_____
_____
_____
_____
_____
_____
_____
_____
_____
_____
_____
_____
_____
_____

151. "You are getting soft."

He rubbed at his stomach looking confused.

"Not that kind of soft."

152. "So, this is the secret lair?"

His brow furrowed. "It's more of a hidey hole. The lair is a hundred miles north.

153. "You know why that terrifies you, don't you?"

"Are you about to spout more of your mumbo jumbo?"

"Fight it if you want; you are doomed to face your past lives."

154. "You could have saved me," the shadowy figure growled.

"I couldn't break protocol...I wanted to—"

More dialogue prompts...

155. "We need to lose this battle to win the war."

"Uh, I think you have that a little mixed up."

He shook his head. "No, I don't. This is why..."

156. "Is this thing going to go off?"

"It depends," he shrugged, way too casually.

157. "What's stage two?"

"I...I didn't plan that far. I didn't think we'd make it."

"What?"

158. "You need to come with me, I've seen your past."

"Yeah, so have I. Are you some sort of fortune teller or something? Never mind, I'm calling the cops."

"No, please. I'm not crazy—I'm here to help."

159. "Prisoner 7649, keep your eyes on the screen. Closing them will result in punishment."

Through clenched teeth, he rasped, "Complying."

160. "Fine, then I want a car."

"Really."

"A nice one. The trunk needs to open with a clicker."

Prompt # _____ Your Title: _____

Fill in the Blank: 49 Possibilities

161. Seconds after the ___, ___ down the stairwell.

Blank One	Blank Two
balloon popped	priests moved
play began	water flooded
alarm blared	fog twisted
power went out	robots raced
public voted	glitter rained
orchestra began	he sprang
buzzer sounded	police in tactical uniforms streamed

162. Books were __ in the __.

Blank One	Blank Two
piled high	smuggling operation
showing debt	grand library
secretly stashed	catacombs, safely hidden from thieves
being burned	maze of buildings
in the cargo container	shelter
hollowed out	hospital
written by children	dusty archives

163. The stainless steel roof __, as people __.

Blank One	Blank Two
hung with ice	sought refuge
thundered with feet	partied to soaring music
groaned under the weight	admired the impressive structure
stopped the balloons	recovered from exposure
kept the rains out	watched the exhibition
sizzled in the dessert sun	enjoyed the birthday celebration
finished the industrial design	kicked to free themselves

164. Water was both (their) __ and (their) __.

Blank One	Blank Two
protection	servant
transportation	life-line
healer	poisoner
rain	destruction
god	feared
bringer of hope	light
worshipped	energy

It's Your Choice

Writing Challenge:

Give your character a secret that influences all of his or her decisions.

Choose Your Noun

man	woman	child	teenager	convict
priest	politician	surfer	student	barista
cow	dog	horse	tiger	kangaroo
dragon	dinosaur	unicorn	mammoth	griffin

165. "Keep that up and you'll be wearing a barbed wire necklace," he warned the ___.

166. The ___ rounded the corner, skidding off to one side, only to slam into the tree.

167. "How many times a day do you need to eat?" she asked the ___.

_____

_____

_____

_____

_____

_____

_____

_____

_____

_____

_____

_____

_____

_____

_____

_____

Choose Your Noun

man	woman	child	teenager	convict
priest	politician	surfer	student	barista
cow	dog	horse	tiger	kangaroo
dragon	dinosaur	unicorn	mammoth	griffin

168. Craggy rocks stretched in every direction, making it difficult for the ___ to travel with any speed.

169. ___s were often seen loitering at the edge of the meadow. If only we had known the real reason they'd been here.

Choose an Exotic Phobia

170. Your character has an exotic phobia—and now they have to face their fear.

Name of Phobia	Fear of
Ailurophobia	cats
Arachibutyrophobia	peanut butter sticking to the roof of your mouth
Belonophobia	pins and needles
Ergasiophobia	writing
Erythrophobia	blushing
Gephydrophobia	crossing bridges
Ophidiophobia	snakes
Pnigophobia	choking
Siderodromophobia	railways
Taphophobia	being buried alive
Triskedekaphobia	the number 13 (especially Friday the 13th)
Pantaphobia	everything

From *Psychology* 3rd edition by Spencer Rathus. New York: Holt, Rinehart & Winston, 1987.

Choose Who and When

171. What if your character was raised by ___ in the year ___.

children	a princess	1550	1620
Martians	a musician	1776	1890
pirates	a shaman	1920	1935
assassins	an inventor	1950	1988
teachers	a transient	1997	2030

That's Classic

Writing Challenge:

Combine three different character archetypes into a single character for a unique blend of traits. There is a chart in the back to help.

Famous Firsts

Use these famous first lines to inspire a totally different story. Avoid using any characters or setting from the source material.

171. "Call me Ishmael." —Herman Melville, *Moby-Dick* (1851)

172. "All happy families are alike; each unhappy family is unhappy in its own way." —*Anna Karenina*, Leo Tolstoy (1878)

173. "All this happened, more or less." —Kurt Vonnegut, *Slaughterhouse-Five* (1969)

174. "It was a bright cold day in April, and the clocks were striking thirteen." —George Orwell, *1984* (1949)

175. "I am a camera with its shutter open, quite passive, recording, not thinking." —Christopher Isherwood, *Goodbye To Berlin'* (1939)

176. "If I am out of my mind, it's all right with me, thought Moses Herzog." —Saul Bellow, *Herzog* (1964)

177. "In my younger and more vulnerable years my father gave me some advice that I've been turning over in my mind ever since." —F. Scott Fitzgerald, *The Great Gatsby* (1925)

178. "I am an invisible man." —Ralph Ellison, *Invisible Man* (1952)

179. "It is a truth universally acknowledged, that a single man in possession of a good fortune, must be in want of a wife." —Jane Austen, *Pride and Prejudice* (1813)

180. "124 was spiteful." —Toni Morrison, *Beloved* (1987)

181. "You better not never tell nobody but God." —Alice Walker, *The Color Purple* (1982)

182. "It was a pleasure to burn." —Ray Bradbury, *Fahrenheit 451* (1953)

183. "It was the best of times, it was the worst of times, it was the age of wisdom, it was the age of foolishness, it was the epoch of belief, it was the epoch of incredulity, it was the season of Light, it was the season of Darkness, it was the spring of hope, it was the winter of despair." —Charles Dickens, *A Tale of Two Cities* (1859)

184. "Mother died today." —Albert Camus, *The Stranger*; translated by Stuart Gilbert (1942)

185. "The past is a foreign country: they do things differently there." —*The Go-Between*, L.P. Hartley (1953)

186. "The sun shone, having no alternative, on the nothing new." —Samuel Beckett, *Murphy* (1938)

187. "A screaming comes across the sky." —Thomas Pynchon, *Gravity's Rainbow* (1973)

188. "Through the fence, between the curling flower spaces, I could see them hitting." —William Faulkner, *The Sound and the Fury* (1929)

189. In a sense, I am Jacob Horner. —John Barth, *The End of the Road* (1958)

Prompt # _____ Your Title: _____

Besties

Your character is best friends with a famous character. Write a short story of adventure and intrigue. *(Notes: Books or films are listed unless the character name matches the series title)*

190. Sherlock Holmes

191. Jo March (*Little Women*)

192. Harry Potter

193. Cleopatra (*Antony & Cleopatra*)

194. Hannibal Lector

195. Mina Harker (*Dracula*)

196. Julius Caesar

197. Elizabeth Bennet (*Pride & Prejudice*)

198. Percy Jackson

199. Anne Shirley (*Anne of Greene Gables*)

200. Romeo Montague (*Romeo & Juliet*)

201. Celie (*The Color Purple*)

202. Indiana Jones

203. Cinderella

204. Darth Vader (*Star Wars*)

205. Jane Eyre

206. Lucy Pevensie (*Narnia*)

207. Hamlet

208. Katniss Everdeen (*The Hunger Games*)

209. Inigo Montoya (*The Princess Bride*)

210. Atticus Finch (*To Kill a Mockingbird*)

211. Mr. Smee (*Peter Pan*)

212. Charlotte (*Charlotte's Web*)

213. Piglet (*Winnie the Pooh*)

214. Daisy Buchanan (*The Great Gatsby*)

215. The Red Ranger (*Power Rangers*)

Prompt # ____ Your Title: _____

Traditional Prompts

Self-Discovery

Many of these are twists on well-worn topics, but creativity can spring from old favorites. These may help unlock something inside yourself, serve as interview questions, or help develop a character background.

216. You can have an extra hand, eye, or foot. What do you choose and why?

217. "Design a Friend" becomes the rage at school. What type of friend would you create?

218. A fairy grants you the ability to see one day in your future. What would you pick? Why?

219. You invent a new type of food. What would it taste like and what could it do for your body?

220. What if you woke up one morning and everyone in your city looked identical?

221. You find the end of the rainbow and are given the pot of gold. What do you do now?

222. In ten years, you will be able to solve a worldwide problem. What problem do you solve and why?

223. You wake up with a passport, a roll of cash, and a toothbrush in your pocket. When you go to the window, you realize you are in a different country and don't speak the language. What do you do?

224. A woman shows up at your house and gives you the opportunity to join an archeological dig for a famous artifact. What are you trying to find and where is it?

225. If you could go on vacation by yourself for one week, where would you go and what would you do?

226. What is the most serious problem at your work or school?

227. You have a secret hideout. Where is it, what is it like, and why do you need it?

228. What happens to people after they die?

229. You come face-to-face with yourself—only to find out that you are one in a set of triplets. Two siblings were stolen away at birth.

230. You have the ability to go back and change one thing in your past. What do you change and how do you rewrite your history? Does it impact your future? If so, what happens?

231. The President asks you to create the next national holiday. What do you create and why? How will it be celebrated? What traditions must be kept?

Prompt # _____ Your Title: _____

If You Were

If you were ___, who/what would you be? Explain by telling a story, using vivid verbs and sensory images.

232. a door stop

233. the bumper on a car

234. a cell phone

235. a diary

236. a climbing rose on a trellis

237. a painting in a museum

238. a mop in a palace

239. a teddy bear

240. a hair ribbon

241. a flashlight

242. fog

243. moonlight

244. a hat

245. a dictionary

246. seaweed

247. an asteroid

248. a coffee mug

249. a mountain peak

250. a well-loved quilt

251. a piece of mail

Vocabulary Upgrade

Remove the word "get/got" and replace it with something more specific.

I <u>got</u> the stapler.

I <u>seized</u> the stapler.

I <u>snatched</u> the stapler.

Can you see how swapping out that one seemingly insignificant word changes everything?

Prompt # _____ Your Title: _____

Mixed Bag

A little mix of everything to keep it interesting.

252. Pandora's Box is real—and it has been opened.

253. Take the main characters from two different fairy or folktales and put them in a futuristic setting.

254. The woman at the end of the street has to leave her cats to save humanity.

255. Your character wakes up in rumpled clothes with a small wooden box next to her/him. A sticky note on top of the box says, "Open to save the world. Keep closed to save yourself."

256. An air raid siren splits the sky—incoming dragons.

257. Your characters have been travelling for days, only to discover that they have been making a huge circle. But, it was because the landscape itself was shifting to keep them there.

258. A teen is given a car on his sixteenth birthday, but it isn't a normal car.

259. A man named Chance enters a small town. Within three days, everyone knows why that is his name.

260. Throughout the night, there is a dripping sound, but it wasn't coming from the faucet.

261. Your character has been losing two hours each day and has no idea what has been happening. While at the post office, he/she sees a wanted poster with his/her face on it, but with a different name.

262. Your character's mother enters the room, sopping with green goo.

263. A device (or drug) allows your character to hear the thoughts of animals, but something goes wrong.

264. Two survivors have three days' worth of food left. Unfortunately, rescue is weeks out.

265. While on a routine flight, a plane disappears for six hours, but never lands. When it reappears, there are three extra passengers.

266. Your character poses as a priest in order to hear the confession of...

267. Your character has been convicted of a crime. As punishment, he/she will lose one of their five senses.

268. Venus and Pluto go on a date, how does it impact the galaxy?

269. Stranded because of a horrible storm, you beg entry into a home in the country. The couple has four children named Summer, Autumn, Winter, and Lucifer. You soon find out why.

270. Your character is hitchhiking across the country. What does he/she experience?

271. Pick an inanimate object in the room with you. Write a story from that object's perspective.

272. You wake up in your favorite childhood cartoon.

273. Describe a character from two points of view: from someone who loves the character and from someone who despises the character.

274. Write the story of the three little pigs from the perspective of the houses.

275. Your character has the ability to learn any language in an hour. The problem is that they can only remember one language at a time.

276. Death gets pulled over for speeding.

277. Your character discovers a box of aged love letters—he/she is the recipient, but the post-date is in the future.

278. Your character transforms into an animal for twelve hours of every day.

279. Pollution levels in all cities rise to the point that everyone must wear a mask outside. What are the impacts of this, both positive and negative?

280. Would you rather have horns, a tale, or hooves? Pick one and use it in a story.

281. An appliance goes crazy in the kitchen and won't stop (dishwasher with too many suds, popcorn maker with limitless popcorn, etc.). Describe the chaos using comedy.

282. The zombie apocalypse is upon us. Write an adventure story using comedy or tragedy.

283. Your character has to relive a day over and over until they solve a crisis. What is the crisis and how will they solve it?

284. The devil's son decides to take a vacation from Hell and falls for a guardian angel.

285. Your character lives in a world where people's eye color changes with their mood, making it almost impossible to lie. Their sensitive eyes can't handle contact lenses.

286. A summer camp for secret agents.

287. A national convention for gremlins is in session. What seminars would they attend?

Locked in

288. You and a friend (or you alone) are locked in __ , with no way out (after hours).

1. a zoo
2. a department store
3. a cabin in the woods
4. a monastery
5. a lighthouse
6. a nuclear bomb shelter
7. a prison
8. an insane asylum
9. an assassin's clubhouse
10. a werewolf den
11. an alien spaceship
12. the White House
13. the Russian embassy
14. a toy store
15. your ex's house
16. the roof of a high-rise building
17. an elementary school
18. a fairy queen's country cottage
19. a serial killer's hideout
20. a forest service shack
21. a condemned theatre
22. the penthouse of a top movie star
23. a medieval cathedral
24. a police station
25. a room with an awkward relative
26. Buckingham Palace
27. Disneyland
28. the Louvre
29. an automotive factory
30. a haunted mansion
31. a junkyard
32. an ancient cemetery
33. the Eiffel Tower
34. a lumber mill
35. a slaughter house
36. an abandoned hospital
37. Dracula's London house
38. Santa's workshop
39. a dentist's office
40. the Vatican
41. a basement
42. a train car
43. an airport
44. a wax museum
45. a decommissioned cruise ship
46. the sewers
47. a submarine
48. a moon base
49. a ski lodge
50. a movie set

289. Up the suspense by adding a complication (or two). Here are some ideas.
- ☐ the security guards aren't really security guards
- ☐ you start feeling sick and wonder if you have been poisoned
- ☐ a gun being cocked nearby
- ☐ your cellphone rings at the wrong time
- ☐ escaped felons are in the area
- ☐ a flash flood warning chimes on your phone
- ☐ pipe organ music fills the room (or area)
- ☐ an earthquake happens, but was it really an earthquake?
- ☐ you blackout for a few minutes and wake with ___ in your hand
- ☐ an inhuman sound in the distance

Prompt # ____ Your Title: _____

Prompt # _____ Your Title: _____

Prompt # _____ Your Title: _____

_____

_____

_____

_____

_____

_____

_____

_____

_____

_____

_____

_____

_____

_____

_____

_____

_____

_____

_____

_____

_____

_____

_____

Prompt # _____ Your Title: _____

Prompt # _____ Your Title: _____

Prompt # _____ Your Title: _____

_____
_____
_____
_____
_____
_____
_____
_____
_____
_____
_____
_____
_____
_____
_____
_____
_____
_____
_____
_____
_____
_____
_____
_____
_____

Prompt # _____ Your Title: _____

Tanka

A Practice in Brevity

Writing Challenge:

Diversify your topics and include haikus: about a friend, a family member, and something romantic. Then tap into some emotions: happiness, sadness, indifference, and need.

Tankas are a great way to practice precise language. They are five lines long. The first line is five syllables, the second is seven, the third is five, the fourth is seven, and the fifth is five (5-7-5-7-5). Here are a couple of samples.

They can be romantic:

Breathless confessions— 5
Joys like brilliant sunshine, 7
Unfurling feeling. 5
Warm brushes of softest lips, 7
True love revealed. 5

—Robin Woods

Or even sinister:

Claws scraping on bone. 5
Dark intentions hide within. 7
Wishes of ill will— 5
wickedness a swirling void. 7
All through smiling teeth. 5

—Robin Woods

290. About love:

_____

_____

_____

_____

_____

291. About loss:

_____

_____

_____

_____

_____

292. About joy:

_____

_____

_____

_____

_____

293. About friendship:

_____

_____

_____

_____

_____

294. About the city:

_____

_____

_____

_____

_____

295. Your choice:

_____

_____

_____

_____

_____

Journal

Writing Challenge:

Use this space as a traditional journal, or for a list of story ideas that were
inspired by the prompts.

Reference

Character Archetypes

Your protagonist and antagonist are usually an amalgam of many character archetypes. The supporting characters tend to function in one of these capacities: the sidekick, love interest, mentor, fool, or nemesis.

If you want your characters to have depth, it is often good to start with an archetype, and then add other characteristics to that character.

Sample Character Archetypes		
Academic	Flatterer (Sycophant)	Politician
Anti-hero	Foil	Priest
Athlete	Fool	Rebel
Bad Boy	Genius	Red Shirt (Cannon Fodder)
Battle Axe	Guardian	Ruler
Black Knight	Hero	Scapegoat (Fall Guy)
Caregiver	Innocent Youth (Ingénue)	Seer
Christ Figure	Jester	Shrew
Courtesan	Loner	Sidekick
Creator	Love Interest	Spoiled Child
Crone	Magician	Temptress
Damsel in Distress	Malcontent	Tomboy
Destroyer	Mentor	Trickster
Dirty Old Man	Miser (Scrooge)	Unwilling Hero
Doppelgänger	Mother Figure	Villain
Explorer	Nemesis	Warrior
Everyman (Commoner)	Old Man	White Knight
Father Figure	Orphan	Wise Elder
Femme Fatale	Outlaw	Young Lover
Other Archetypes:		

Character Motivations

In order to have a well-rounded character, they should have multiple reasons that motivate them to do the things they do. No character is purely good or evil, but a mixture of both.

Reasons for Characters to Act			
Acceptance	Disgust	Justice	Rage
Adventure	Duty	Knowledge	Rebellion
Alienation	Eagerness	Legacy	Reconciliation
Ambition	Empathy	Loneliness	Redemption
Anxiety	Envy	Loss	Regret
Avoidance	Escape	Love	Religion
Career	Failure	Lust	Resentment
Catastrophe	Fame	Money	Resolution
Codependence	Fear	Morality	Revenge
Comfort	Friends	Outrage	Rivalry
Compassion	Frustration	Peer Pressure	Satisfaction
Contempt	Glory	Perfectionism	Self-Improvement
Contentment	Greed	Persecution	Shame
Control	Grief	Pity	Sickness
Corruption	Guilt	Pleasure	Stubbornness
Credit	Hate	Popularity	Survival
Curiosity	Honor	Power	Thrills
Cursed	Horror	Prejudice	Torment
Debt	Hurt	Prestige	Valor
Desperation	Ideology	Pride	Vengeance
Destiny	Infatuation	Protection	War
Discovery	Insanity	PTSD	Wrath

Other:

Voice Descriptors

Words to Describe
Voice

aggressive
airy
angelic
appealing
articulate
blubbery
breathy
brittle
calloused
clipped
crisp
croaky
dead
disembodied

droning
ethereal
flat
fluttery
froggy
fussy
garbled
glib
grating
gravelly
gruff
guttural
harsh
high

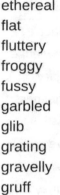

honey
husky
insincere
low
matter-of-fact
mewling
monotone
musical
nagging
nasal
purr
quacking
quaking
quivering
quiet
raspy
ringing
robotic
rough
rumbling
seething
shrill
silky
silvery
singsong
slinky

slithery
small
smoky
smooth
snarly
snippy
sniveling
sour
strangled
strident
stuttering
sugary
taut
thin
throaty
tight
trilling
weak
weedy
wheezy
whiney
wobbly
wooden
worn
yappy
yippy

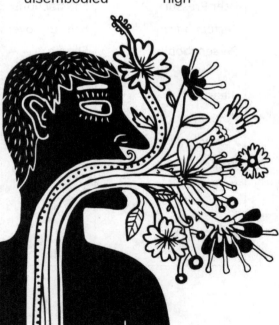

Character Traits

All characters, even good ones, should have some reasonable flaws. And in turn, characters that are purely evil often appear fake. It is best to have a healthy mix of believable traits. Here is a list to get you thinking:

Positive Traits

Adaptable	Accepting	Adventurous	Affectionate	Amiable
Alert	Astute	Benevolent	Brave	Charismatic
Creative	Decisive	Dependable	Diplomatic	Disciplined
Earnest	Efficient	Empathetic	Enthusiastic	Ethical
Fair	Forgiving	Good-Hearted	Gracious	Happy
Hard-Working	Independent	Insightful	Intelligent	Just
Leader	Loving	Nurturing	Orderly	Patient
Passionate	Persuasive	Playful	Responsible	Resourceful
Self-Aware	Spunky	Strong	Studious	Supportive
Tactful	Tenacious	Unselfish	Watchful	Wise

Negative Traits

Abusive	Addictive	Aggressive	Antisocial	Apathetic
Argumentative	Belligerent	Callous	Cantankerous	Childish
Clingy	Closed-Minded	Cocky	Compulsive	Cowardly
Cruel	Cynical	Dangerous	Deceitful	Defensive
Degrading	Destructive	Disloyal	Egocentric	Evil
Fearful	Fixated	Flaky	Foolish	Forgetful
Hostile	Hung-Up	Insecure	Loner	Megalomaniacal
Neurotic	Phobic	Perfectionist	Pessimistic	Prejudiced
Manipulative	Selfish	Self-Destructive	Stubborn	Sulker
Touchy	Unreceptive	Vengeful	Whiney	Withdrawn

Character Appearance Charts

Eye Color					
	Blue	Sky Blue	Baby Blue	Electric Blue	Cornflower
	Brown	Chestnut	Chocolate	Cognac	Amber
	Green	Sea Green	Moss Green	Jade	Emerald
	Grey	Silver	Gunmetal Grey	Charcoal	Black
	Hazel	Russet	Nut	Honey	Yellow
	Lavender	Other:			

Eye Shape					
	Almond	Round	Drooping	Hooded	Close-Set
	Wide-Set	Deep-Set	Protruding	Sleepy	Squinting
	Down-Turned	Other:			

Skin Tone					
	Fair	Ivory	Porcelain	Milky	Snow
	Ruddy	Rose	Peach	Ochre	Golden
	Olive	Khaki	Toffee	Honey	Tawny
	Dark	Ebony	Sepia	Russet	Mahogany
	Other:				

Body Shape					
	Triangle	Rectangle	Hourglass	Rounded	Diamond
	Inverted Triangle	Barrel	Willowy	Husky	Wiry
	Other:				

Facial Shapes					
	Oval	Rectangle	Square	Heart	Oblong
	Egg	Diamond	Triangle	Narrow	Block-Like
	Other:				

Hair Color					
	Black	Dark Brown	Medium Brown	Ash Brown	Golden Brown
	Red	Auburn	Copper	Strawberry	Cinnamon
	Blond	Platinum	White	Silver	Grey
	Other:				

Notes:

Words for Sounds

Add appeal to your writing by making a splash with descriptive sound words.

Ahem	Clatter	Grind	Pound	Splash	Tweet
Baa	Click	Groan	Pow	Splat	Vroom
Babble	Clink	Gulp	Pulsing	Splinter	Wail
Bang	Clomp	Gurgle	Purr	Sputter	Wallop
Bark	Clonk	Guzzle	Quack	Squawk	Whack
Beat	Clop	Hammer	Racket	Squeak	Wheeze
Beep	Cluck	Hiss	Rap	Squish	Whicker
Bellow	Clunk	Hoot	Ratchet	Stomp	Whinny
Blare	Crackle	Howl	Rattle	Suck	Whip
Blast	Crash	Hubbub	Revved	Swish	Whir
Blip	Creak	Hum	Ring	Swoop	Whisper
Blop	Crinkle	Jangle	Rip	Swoosh	Whistle
Blow	Crunch	Jingle	Roar	Tap	Whiz
Boing	Din	Kerplunk	Rumble	Tatter	Woof
Bong	Ding	Knock	Rushing	Tee-Hee	Woot
Boo	Discord	Lash	Rustle	Throb	Yap
Boom	Drip	Mew	Scream	Thud	Yawp
Bop	Drone	Mewl	Screech	Thump	Yelp
Bray	Drum	Murmur	Scuff	Thunder	Yip
Bubble	Eek	Neigh	Shriek	Thwack	Yowl
Burp	Fanfare	Oink	Shuffle	Tick	Zap
Buzz	Fizz	Ooze	Sizzle	Tinkle	Zip
Cacophony	Fizzle	Patter	Slam	Titter	Zoom
Cha-Ching	Flick	Peal	Slap	Tock	
Cheep	Fling	Peep	Slop	Tolling	Other:
Chime	Flop	Pew	Slurp	Toot	
Chirp	Fracas	Pitter-Patter	Smack	Trill	
Chug	Giggle	Plink	Snap	Tromp	
Clack	Glug	Plod	Snicker	Trumpet	
Clamor	Glurp	Plop	Snigger	Tsk	
Clang	Gnashing	Plunk	Snip	Tumult	
Clank	Gobble	Poof	Snort	Tut	
Clap	Grating	Pop	Spatter	Twang	

Number Symbolism

Choosing numbers that have symbolic meaning and weight can add depth to your narrative. We see it in literature all the time—three little pigs, seven dwarves, etc.

Popular Symbolic Numbers	
Two	Duality, partnership, male & female, yin & yang, left & right, hot & cold, sun & moon, night & day, active & passive, other:
Three	Trinity (Father, Son, & Holy Spirit), circle of life (birth, life, & death), idea of self (mind, body, & spirit), mystical number in folktales (three wishes, three challenges, three guesses, etc.), three rulers in Greek mythology (Zeus, Hades, & Poseidon), three Fates, Shakespeare's *Macbeth* has three witches, other:
Four	Four elements (earth, air, wind, & fire), four cardinal points (north, south, east, & west), humanity (four limbs), four seasons, four humors (blood, choler, phlegm, & black bile), four phases of the moon, four horseman of the Apocalypse, other:
Six	Satan, evil, the devil (666 is the biblical "mark of the devil"), other:
Seven	Trinity plus humanity (3+4), days of the week, seven deadly sins, other:
Nine	Nine lives of a cat, Norse mythology there are nine worlds, Greek mythology there are nine Muses, other:
Twelve	A complete cycle, twelve months, twelve hours, twelve disciples of Christ, twelve tribes of Israel, twelve inches in a foot, other:
Thirteen	Unlucky, bad luck, Judas was the thirteenth person to arrive to the last supper, other:
Forty	Trials and tribulations, Hebrews wandered for forty years, other:
Notes:	

Tastes and Aromas

When you are writing, try to incorporate all four of the senses in your work. Here is a cheat sheet for tastes and smells:

Positive	Neutral	Negative	Spices	Florals (Most Fragrant)
Aromatic	Acidic	Biting	Cajun	Angel's Trumpet
Citrusy	Acrid	Bitter	Cinnamon	Flowering Plum
Comforting	Airy	Decay	Clove	Heliotrope
Crisp	Ancient	Dirty	Coriander	Honeysuckle
Delicate	Brackish	Fetid	Cumin	Jasmin
Delicious	Burnt	Foul	Dill	Lavender
Exquisite	Delicate	Funky	Pepper	Lilac
Fragrant	Feminine	Gamy	Sage	Mexican Orange
Fresh	Fermented	Harsh	Thyme	Mock Orange
Fruity	Masculine	Moldy	Basil	Rose
Full-Bodied	Floral	Musty	Barbeque	Star Magnolia
Hard	Humid	Nasty	Bay Leaf	Sweet Peas
Heady	Light	Noxious	Curry	Tuberose
Juicy	Medicinal	Old	Anise	
Lemony	Medium	Pungent	Caraway Seed	**Household Smells**
Rich	Mellow	Putrid	Cardamom	
Savory	Metallic	Rancid	Cayenne	Babies
Sharp	Mild	Rank	Cumin	"Boy" Smell
Succulent	Minty	Repulsive	Dill	Bacon
Sugary	Moist	Rotting	Fennel	BBQ
Sweet	Musky	Skunky	Garlic	Beer
Tangy	Nippy	Sour	Ginger	Books
Tart	Nutty	Spoiled	Mace	Bread
Tempting	Peppery	Stagnant	Marjoram	Burning Wood
Warm	Perfumed	Stale	Mint	Chocolate
Woody	Salty	Stench	Mustard	Cinnamon
Zesty	Woodsy	Stinking	Onion	Citrus
Zingy	Yeasty	Stuffy	Orange Peel	Coconut
			Lemon Peel	Coffee
Other:	Other:	Other:	Nutmeg	Cut Grass
			Rosemary	Dirty Laundry
			Saffron	Fresh–Baked Cookies
			Turmeric	Fresh Laundry
			Vanilla	Pine
				Soap

Synonyms

As you are editing, it is important to pay attention to repetition. Much of the tinkering with words will come with editing, but I love using synonym sheets to cut down on the editing later, as well as to inspire me.

Emotions

Other words for **Happy**

Alluring, amused, appealing, appeased, blissful, blithe, carefree, charmed, cheeky, chipper, chirpy, content, convivial, delighted, elated, electrified, ecstatic, enchanted, enthusiastic, exultant, excited, fantastic, fulfilled, glad, gleeful, glowing, gratified, idyllic, intoxicating, jolly, joyful, joyous, jovial, jubilant, light, lively, merry, mirthful, overjoyed, pleased, pleasant, radiant, sparkling, savoured, satisfied, serene, sunny, thrilled, tickled, up, upbeat, winsome, wonderful.

Other words for **SAD**

Aching, agitated, anguished, anxious, bleak, bothered, brooding, bugged, chagrined, cheerless, darkly, disillusioned, disappointed, disenchanted, disheartened, dismayed, distraught, dissatisfied, despondent, doleful, failed, faint, frustrated, glazed, gloomy, glowering, haunted, hopeless, languid, miserable, pained, perturbed, sour, suffering, sullen, thwarted, tormented, troubled, uneasy, unsettled, upset, vacant, vexed, wan, woeful, wounded.

Other words for **Mad**

Affronted, aggravated, agitated, angered, annoyed, bitter, boiling, bothered, brooding, bugged, bummed, cantankerous, chafed, chagrined, crabby, cross, disgruntled, distraught, disturbed, enflamed, enraged, exasperated, fiery, fuming, furious, frantic, galled, goaded, hacked, heated, hostile, hot, huffy, ill-tempered, incensed, indignant, inflamed, infuriated, irate, ireful, irritated, livid, maddened, malcontent, miffed, nettled, offended, peeved, piqued, provoked, raging, resentful, riled, scowling, sore, sour, stung, taut, tense, tight, troubled, upset, vexed, wrathful.

Other words for **Crying**

Bawling, blubbering, gushing, howling, lamenting, moaning, scream-crying, silent tears, sniffling, snivelling, sobbing, sorrowing, teary, wailing, weepy, woeful.

Commonly Used Words

Other words for ASKED

Appealed, begged, beckoned, beseeched, besieged, bid, craved, commanded, claimed, coaxed, challenged, charged, charmed, cross-examined, demanded, drilled, entreated, enchanted, grilled, implored, imposed, interrogated, invited, invoked, inquired, insisted, needled, ordered, pleaded, petitioned, picked, probed, pried, pressed, pumped, pursued, put through the wringer, put the screws down, questioned, queried, quizzed, requested, required, requisitioned, roasted, solicited, summoned, surveyed, sweated, urged, wanted, wheedled, wooed, worried, wondered.

Other words for LAUGH

Break up, burst, cackle, chortle, chuckle, crack-up, crow, giggle, grin, guffaw, hee-haw, howl, peal, quack, roar, scream, shriek, snicker, snigger, snort, split one's sides, tee-hee, titter, whoop.

Other Words for LOOK

Address, admire, attention, audit, babysit, beam, beholding, blink, bore, browse, burn, cast, check, comb, consider, contemplate, delve, detect, discover, disregard, distinguish, ensure, evil eye, examine, explore, eye, eyeball, ferret, fix, flash, forage, gander, gaze, get an eyeful, give the eye, glance, glare, glaze, glimmer, glimpse, glitter, gloat, goggle, grope, gun, have a gander, inquire, inspect, investigate, judge, keeping watch, leaf-through, leer, lock daggers on, look fixedly, look-see, marking, moon, mope, neglect, note, notice, noting, observe, ogle, once-over, peek, peep, peer, peg, peruse, poke into, scan, pout, probe, pry, quest, rake, recognize, reconnaissance, regard, regarding, renew, resemble, review, riffle, rubberneck, rummage, scan, scowl, scrutinize, search, seeing, sense, settle, shine, sift, simper, size-up, skim, slant, smile, smirk, snatch, sneer, speculative, spot, spy, squint, stare, study, sulk, supervise, surveillance, survey, sweep, take stock of, take in, trace, verify, view, viewing, watch, witness, yawp, zero in.

Other words for REPLIED

Acknowledged, answered, argued, accounted, barked, bit, be in touch, boomeranged, comeback, countered, conferred, claimed, denied, echoed, feedback, fielded the question, get back to, growled, matched, parried, reacted, reciprocated, rejoined, responded, retorted, remarked, returned, retaliated, shot back, snapped, squelched, squared, swung, vacillated.

Other words for **Sat**

Be seated, bear on, cover, ensconce, give feet a rest, grab a chair, have a place, have a seat, hunker, install, lie, park, perch, plop down, pose, posture, put it there, relax, remain, rest, seat, seat oneself, settle, squat, take a load off, take a place, take a seat.

Other words for **Was/Were**   VERB (TO BE)

Abided, acted, be alive, befell, breathed, continued, coexisted, do, endured, ensued, existed, had been, happened, inhabited, lasted, lived, moved, obtained, occurred, persisted, prevailed, remained, rested, stood, stayed, survived, subsided, subsisted, transpired.

Other words for **Walk**

Advance, amble, barge, bolt, bounce, bound, canter, charge, crawl, creep, dance, dash, escort, gallop, hike, hobble, hop, jog, jump, leap, limp, lope, lumber, meander, mosey, move, pad, pace march, parade, patrol, plod, prance, proceed, promenade, prowl, race, roam, rove, run, sashay, saunter, scamper, scramble, zip shuffle, skip, slink, slither, slog, sprint, stagger, step, stomp, stride, stroll, strut, stumble, swagger, thread, tiptoe, traipse, tramp, tread, trek, trip, trot, trudge, wade, wander.

Other words for **Whisper**

Breathed, buzz, disclosed, exhaled, expressed, fluttered, gasped, hint, hiss, hum, hushed tone, intoned, lament, low voice, moaned, mouthed, mumble, murmur, mutter, puff, purred, reflected, ruffle, rumble, rush, said low, said softly, sigh, sob, undertone, utter, voiced, wheezed.

Other words for **Went**

Abscond, ambled, approached, avoided, be off, beat it, bolted, bounced, bounded, bugged out, burst, carved, cleared out, crawled, crept, cruised, cut and run, danced, darted, dashed, decamped, deserted, disappeared, ducked out, escaped, evaded, exited, fared, fled, floated, flew, flew the coop, galloped, got away, got going, got lost, glided, go down, go south, hightailed, hit the road, hoofed it, hopped, hotfooted, hurdled, hustled, journeyed, jumped, leapt, left, lighted out, loped, lunged, made haste, made a break for it, made for, made off, made tracks, marched, moseyed, moved, muscled, neared, negotiated, paced, paraded, passed, pedalled, proceeded, progressed, pulled out, pulled, pushed off, pushed on, quitted, retired, retreated, rode, ran along, ran away, rushed, sashayed, scampered, scooted, scrammed, scurried, scuttled, set off, set out, shot, shouldered, shoved off, shuffled, skedaddled, skipped out, skipped, skirted, slinked, slipped, soared, split, sprang, sprinted, stole away, steered clear, stepped on it, strolled, strutted, scurried, swept, took a hike, took a powder, took flight, took leave, took off, threaded, toddled, tottered, trampled, travelled, traversed, trekked, trode, trudged, tumbled, vamoosed, vanished, vaulted, veered, walked off, wandered, weaved, wended, whisked, withdrew, wormed, zipped, zoomed.

Other words for SAID

Accused, acknowledged, added, announced, addressed, admitted, advised, affirmed, agreed, asked, avowed, asserted, answered, apologized, argued, assured, approved, articulated, alleged, attested, barked, bet, bellowed, babbled, begged, bragged, began, bawled, bleated, blurted, boomed, broke in, bugged, boasted, bubbled, beamed, burst out, believed, brought out, confided, crowed, coughed, cried, congratulated, complained, conceded, chorused, concluded, confessed, chatted, convinced, chattered, cheered, chided, chimed in, clucked, coaxed, commanded, cautioned, continued, commented, called, croaked, chuckled, claimed, choked, chortled, corrected, communicated, claimed, contended, criticized, construe,

dared, decided, disagreed, described, disclosed, drawled, denied, declared, demanded, divulged, doubted, denied, disputed, dictated, echoed, ended, exclaimed, explained, expressed, enunciated, expounded, emphasized, formulated, fretted, finished, gulped, gurgled, gasped, grumbled, groaned, guessed, gibed, giggled, greeted, growled, grunted, hinted, hissed, hollered, hypothesized, inquired, imitated, implied, insisted, interjected, interrupted, intoned, informed, interpreted, illustrated, insinuated, jeered, jested, joked, justified, lied, laughed, lisped, maintained, muttered, marveled, moaned, mimicked, mumble, modulated, murmured, mused, mentioned, mouthed, nagged, noted, nodded, noticed,

objected, observed, offered, ordered, owned up, piped, pointed out, panted, pondered, praised, prayed, puzzled, proclaimed, promised, proposed, protested, purred, pled, pleaded, put in, prevailed, parried, pressed, put forward, pronounced, pointed out, prescribed, popped off, persisted, protested, questioned, quavered, quipped, quoted, queried, rejected, reasoned, ranted, reassured, reminded, responded, recalled, returned, requested, roared, related, remarked, replied, reported, revealed, rebutted, retorted, repeated, reckoned, remembered, regarded, recited, resolved, reflected, ripped, rectified, reaffirmed,

snickered, sniffed, smirked, snapped, snarled, shot, sneered, sneezed, started, stated, stormed, sobbed, stuttered, suggested, surmised, sassed, sputtered, sniffled, snorted, spoke, stammered, squeaked, sassed, scoffed, scolded, screamed, shouted, sighed, smiled, sang, shrieked, shrilled, speculated, supposed, settled, solved, shot back, swore, stressed, spilled, told, tested, trilled, taunted, teased, tempted, theorized, threatened, tore, uttered, unveiled, urged, upheld, vocalized, voiced, vindicated, volunteered, vowed, vented, verbalized, warned, wailed, went on, wept, whimpered, whined, wondered, whispered, worried, warranted, yawned, yakked.

My Synonym Lists:

Other Notes & Research

Books by Robin Woods

Fiction

Allure: A Watcher Series Prequel

The Unintended: The Watcher Series Book One

The Nexus: The Watcher Series Book Two

The Sacrifice: The Watcher Series Book Three

The Fallen: Part One: The Watcher Series Book Four

The Fallen: Part Two: The Watcher Series Book Five

Non-fiction

Fiction Writing Workbook & Journal

Prompt Me Workbook & Journal

Books by Robin Woods

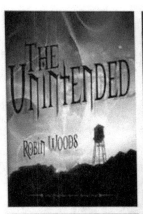

Robin Woods is a high school and university instructor with over two decades of experience teaching English, literature, and writing. She has earned a BA in English and an MA in education.

In addition to teaching, Robin Woods has published six highly-rated novels and has multiple projects in the works, including writing for a Hollywood producer.

When Ms. Woods isn't teaching or writing, she is chasing her two elementary school kids around and spending time with her ever-patient husband.

For more information and free resources, go to her website at:

www.RobinWoodsFiction.com

CPSIA information can be obtained
at www.ICGtesting.com
Printed in the USA
LVHW101950111218
600076LV00002B/53/P

9 781941 077115